How To Voice Standards At The Piano: THE MENU

by Mark Levine

Editors:
Deborah Craig
and Peter Blommers
Special thanks to Chuck Sher

Graphic Design and Cover Art by Attila Nagy, Santa Rosa, California
©2014 SHER MUSIC CO., P.O. Box 445, Petaluma, CA 94953
All Rights Reserved. International Copyright Secured. Made in the USA.
ISBN 1-883217-80-6

For Norma & Rosie

Special thanks to my Teachers:

Joe Pace

Jaki Byard

Hall Overton

Herb Pomeroy

Barry Harris

table of contents

chapter one: the menu

There is a reason why jazz harmony is called jazz *theory* instead of jazz *truth*. The only *truth* is in the music itself. Theory is an intellectual dance we do around the music, trying to explain what's happening and why one thing sounds beautiful to some of us, and another sounds terrible.

This book shows my own approach to voicing standard songs composed by masters like Duke Ellington, Billy Strayhorn, George Gershwin, Cole Porter, and so on.

Some voicings could also be considered standard. Two jazz pianists, one in New York the other in Shanghai, will likely play the same left-hand voicing for D-7. Only a few are played often enough to be thought of as "standard": *left-hand voicings, upper structures, fourth chords, So What chords, stacked thirds, the Kenny Barron Chord,* and so on. You will need to practice all of these chords separately, in every key, to gain the skill you'll need to play them intuitively.

About notation

The 6th and 13th are the same note. 6th is notated on major and minor chords, the 13th on a dominant chord. The 4th and 11th are the same note, used about equally. I notate major seventh chords as "C." Many jazz musicians notate it as CΔ. Take your choice, but be able to understand someone else's choices!

ALICE IN WONDERLAND

"Alice in Wonderland"[1] is a song by Sammy Fain and Bob Hilliard.[2] **Figure 1-1** shows a lead sheet of the tune, with the changes that I usually use. Different pianists use different sets of chords in standards, and this may not match the lead sheet of the ones you might have.[3]

Later in this chapter we will break the song up into smaller sections. Bars 1-4, for example, indicates just the melody and chord symbol. Bars 1-4a indicates the same, plus the addition of the correct chords from the Menu.

---

1   I will abbreviate the title of the song as "Alice" in the text.
2   Copyright 1951 Walt Disney Music Co. All Rights Reserved. Reprinted by Permission.
3   Listen to Bill Evans' version, on The Complete Village Vanguard Recordings, 1961.

Figure 1-1
PIANO

ALICE IN WONDERLAND

Music by Sammy Fain
Lyric by Bob Hilliard

THE VOICINGS

The Menu shows the available voicings you will need to play "Alice." Fold down a corner of this page, bookmark it, or photocopy it, as you will be referring back to it regularly.

Left-hand Voicings

On the first line of The Menu are the *left-hand voicings.*[4] In these voicings, the entire weight of the chord is carried by the left hand, leaving your right hand to either play the melody or improvise.[5] The left-hand voicing played will work with the melody note that is shown in the lead sheet of the tune.

Left-hand Voicings come in two positions: "A" and "B." If you drop into a jazz club from Chicago to Mexico City, you'll hear the jazz pianist play both the "A" and "B" positions a lot. You will notice that all six voicings are *rootless.* There is no "D" in the D-7 chord, and no "G" in the G7 chord. There is a "C" in the C major chord, but its not the bottom note, where the root is traditionally found.

Play them several times until you get used to *hearing them* as rootless chords. And practice them in all 12 keys.

All voicings shown below the left-hand voicings are two-handed voicings. Left-hand voicings and two-handed voicings are coequal – they both sound fine, either separately or combined in playing a tune. You can play entire tunes just using left-hand voicings, and they will sound fine. This book gives prominence to two-handed voicings, because the more notes you play, the more colors you have, and they sound fuller.

So What chords

On the second line of The Menu are the *So What Chords.*[6] Bill Evans played this voicing prominently on Miles Davis' important recording of the song of the same name.[7]

The four chords shown are all the same, with an extra doubled "C" on top in the third and fourth bars. Instead of memorizing them by their positions in a D-7 chord (root - 4th - 7th - 3rd - 5th), its much simpler to look at the intervals between the notes. From the bottom up, the intervals are 4th- 4th- 4th- major 3rd. That's much easier than memorizing their position in the chord itself. After practice, your hands will automatically shape themselves to the chord. This type of learning by feel is called *muscle memory.* Practice them around the *Cycle of 5ths.*

---

4   Abbreviated as "LHV" in the music.
5   The "B" position of left-hand voicings are shown in the treble clef, but are played by the left hand.
6   Abbreviated as "SW" in the music.
7   Miles Davis, *Kind of Blue,* Columbia Records.

The Cycle of 5ths is shown here:

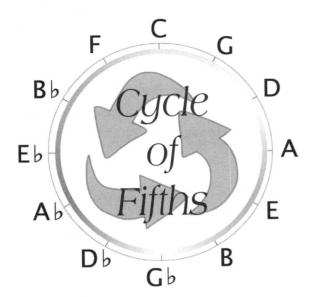

Jazz musicians use the cycle of 5ths to practice, because it follows the direction of most harmony found in standards and jazz tunes. Unlike classical musicians, we go around the cycle *counterclockwise*.

Look at the roots of a II-V-I progression, D-7, G7, C. D, G, and C, [8] follow each other *counterclockwise* around the cycle. I had a dickens of a time drilling this into my students' heads while teaching for a couple of years at the San Francisco Conservatory of Music. They had all learned the cycle *clockwise*. Their usual reaction was "we already know it clockwise, so why should we learn it *counterclockwise?"*

As an example, the roots of the first few chords of the standard "All The Things You Are" are F-7, Bb-7, Eb7, AbΔ, DbΔ...five chords in a row (F, Bb, Eb, Ab, Db) whose roots follow counterclockwise around the cycle. See **FIGURE 1-3**. So when you are learning a new voicing, practice it *counterclockwise*.

FIGURE 1-3   ALL THE THINGS YOU ARE   JEROME KERN

---

8 Many jazz musicians notate a major chord as "CΔ." Because "C" can indicate either a
   C major seventh chord and a C69 chord, I opt for the single letter "C".

Another tip: don't wiggle your fingers as you go from the same voicing to the next one. *The voicing will feel the same no matter what key you are in.* You may pivot your hand when changing a black key to a white key, but your fingers still retain the same shape. *Muscle memory,* or *tactile memory* is what lodges in your brain.

Notice that the same voicing can be used on two different chords: D-7 and Bb. D-7 has a "D" in the root and the 5th in the melody, as that's the way it is usually played on a D-7 chord. The same voicing also works as a rootless Bb, with "A," the major 7th now in the melody.

In the third bar, the added "C" is now the minor 7th of a D-7 chord, and in the fourth bar, the extra C is now the 9th of the Bb chord. Don't think for a moment that a bass player's note determines whether the chord is intended to be D-7 or Bb. I find that it sounds like either, or both, and your audience won't start throwing things at you, whether or not you're playing with a bass player.

Fourth Chords

Now look at the third line of The Menu. These are the *Fourth Chords*,[9] so called because they are made up entirely of *diatonic fourths. "Diatonic"* means "in the key," as all of the chords shown here are in the key of C. Each chord is made up of 4ths, but one of them, between the 4th and 7th notes of the C major scale (F and B in this case), is an *augmented 4th*, better known as a *tritone.[10]*

In the Menu there are seven fourth chords on this line, some played more often than others. Oddly enough, the root of the chord is usually the top note. The first one shows perfect 4ths extending upward from E, the 3rd of a C major chord, to C, the root, on top. If you're playing a song with the root in the melody of a major chord, as the Eb on the first chord in "On Green Dolphin St," or as the C on the first chord of "What's New?" (**FIGURE 1-4**), this is an ideal voicing.

---

9   Abbreviated as "4ths," in the music, not to be confused with "4th," a note in a chord.
10 An ancient musical term, denoting an interval made up of three whole-steps.

Back to the The Menu, Fourth Chords line

Notice that there is a "5" next to G in this chord, as G is the 5th in a C major chord. *Fourth chords* are so spread out that omitting the note on top creates a good voicing for a C major chord with the 5th in the melody: only four notes, but a very full sounding chord.

The third and fourth chords on the *Fourth Chords* line are the same voicing, because they will work on two different chords, D-6 and G7. Notice that on the D-6 version either the root on top or the 5th on top works. On the G7 version, either the 5th on top or the 9th on top works. (Remember, there is a tritone in these voicings, between F and B, but it is still a *diatonic* fourth.) And again, don't worry about the bass player. When you're playing with one, if he or she plays either the G or D in the bass, it won't make any difference. Bass players don't play the roots of chords all the time.

In the fifth bar of the *fourth chords* is a *sus chord.* This chord is associated with Carole King, Stevie Wonder and others in pop music of the 1960 and 1970s, but was first popularized in jazz by Herbie Hancock on his classic song "Maiden Voyage"[11] in the 1970s. This is an unusual voicing for a sus chord, made up entirely of 4ths, with the 13th in the melody. It can also be played as a four-note chord, with the 3rd in the melody. Just omit the top note.

Note also that this "sus" chord has a B, the major 3rd of the Gsus chord. It is a well-known myth that "the 4th takes the place of the 3rd in a sus chord," or "don't ever play a major 3rd in a sus chord!" If you doubt that, listen to Herbie Hancock playing an Ebsus chord on the bridge of *Maiden Voyage,* with G, the 3rd, on the top of the voicing.

In the sixth bar of the *fourth chords* is a six-note chord, G7, a voicing often played as the first chord in a blues. Because this chord voicing has six notes, any of the top three notes: G (the root), D (the 5th), or A (the 9th) can serve as the melody. So the chord can be played as a four- five- or six-note chord.

The 4th voicing in the last bar on the *fourth chord* line is the same as the voicing for Gsus in the fifth bar, but with an additional 4th on top: A, the 9th of the chord.

Upper Structures

Now look at the line of The Menu called *Upper Structures.*[12] These came into prominence in jazz piano back in the 1950s, as played by Bill Evans and Wynton Kelly[13]. They consist of the 3rd and 7th, or *tritone* of a dominant 7th chord, with a triad

---

11 Herbie Hancock, *Maiden Voyage,* Blue Note Records, 1965.
12 Abbreviated as US in the music.
13 On Miles Davis' *"Someday My Prince Will Come,"* Columbia Records.

superimposed on top. They are played on dominant chords with alterations[14] that is, dominant chords with at least one alteration (b9, +9, +4, or b13), often with more than one. Upper structures are kind of backwards: the most delicate and unstable interval, the *tritone,* is on the bottom, while the strongest and most robust chord, a major triad, is on the top. The overtone series can play havoc with this instability, which you must pay attention to when problems arise (more on this below).

First, look at the Roman numeral underneath each chord: the first chord, played on a C7+4, has a II underneath it. That is because the *root* of the triad, D, is a major second above the *root* of the notated chord (C7+4). Hence "II." Roman numerals differentiate between different upper structure chords.

In addition, the 3rd and 7th on the bottom of the voicing can be reversed, putting the 7th on the bottom and the 3rd on top.[15] Furthermore, because triads can be played in three different positions – root position, first inversion, and second inversion – any of the three notes of the triad can be used as a melody note. **FIGURE 1-5** shows a C7+4 chord with five choices to harmonize a melody note. Either the 13th, +4, 9th, or 13th can be in the melody. See how the left hand *tritone* is reversed, first with the 3rd on the bottom, then the 7th, as the chord rises on your piano. Both left hand and right hand need to be fairly close together for *upper structures* to sound good.

FIGURE 1-5   UPPER STRUCTURE CHORD "II" IN VARIOUS POSITIONS

Notice also that the space between your hands is kept small, never more than a 4th, because if it increases by anything more than that, the chord will sound somewhat empty. In addition, if the melody note is played high on the piano (as it is in the last bar on the line), it needs to be doubled, to avoid a tinny, "music box" effect, and to get a fuller sound (see fifth bar of Figure 1-5). So a pianist has five different choices to use these voicings with a melody note on a dominant chord with a +4.

---

14 Not to be confused with the "alt" chord.
15 Shown as both in Figure 1-5.

In The Menu, note that the *upper structure* voicing in the last bar has a *lower case*[16] Roman numeral below it, because it has an F# *minor* triad on top.

A Few Other Voicings

The last line of The Menu shows three different voicings: *Stacked 3rds, the Kenny Barron chord,* and the *Everything chord.*

Stacked 3rds is just that: Play the root of a minor 7th chord in your left hand and add 3rds above it, all white notes because D-7 is in the key of C. The top note is "G," the 4th of a D-7 chord. This chord is often played on a minor 7th chord with the 4th in the melody. Remember, the fourth and eleventh are interchangeable terms: they both mean the same note.

The *Kenny Barron chord*[17] is another option to play on a minor 7th chord with the 4th in the melody, but is much more spread out. Rather than memorize each note's position in the D-7 chord (root, 5th, 9th, 3rd, 7th, 4th), look at your hands as you play this chord. Both your left and right hands are playing two perfect 5ths, with a half-step between your thumbs. When learning to find this chord, aim your left hand little finger at the root, your right hand little finger at the 4th, and the other notes will fall naturally on the correct notes in the middle. Again, *muscle memory.*

The *Everything chord* in the very last bar of The Menu contains all seven notes in the *altered scale,* and is played on an *alt chord*[18] with the root in the melody.

VOICING "ALICE IN WONDERLAND"

Now look at **FIGURE 1-6**, another view of "Alice." One additional item has been added to the lead sheet of "Alice" shown in *Figure 1-1*. To the right of each melody note is a number denoting its place in the chord (root, 9th, 3rd, and so on).

---

16 "iv minor" instead of "IV."

17 After the great pianist Kenny Barron.

18 The alt chord and alt scale are built off of the 7th mode from the *melodic minor* scale, a type of scale and harmony very different from the major scale, and explored more fully in Appendix I.

FIGURE 1-6

ALICE IN WONDERLAND

Music by Sammy Fain
Lyric by Bob Hilliard

Now look at the first four bars, **Bars 1-4.** The first chord is D-7, and the first note in the melody is G, the 4ᵗʰ of D-7. Again, these are the first two notes (D & G) that count.

BARS 1-4

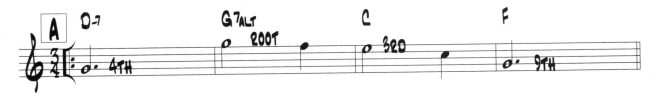

These are the two things to keep in mind so you can proceed,
- the *melody note*
- the *root of the chord.*

Look down The Menu until you see any minor 7th chord symbol with the designation "4ᵗʰ" just to the right of the melody note. The chord voicing shown will be one of the best *two-handed* ones to play on that chord. It's the one shown in the first bar of the last line, labeled *Stacked 3rds,* so-called because it consists of notes stacked in *3rds.:* D, F, A, C, E, G, all white notes.

The voicing just to the right of Stacked 3rds is also a minor 7ᵗʰ chord with the 4ᵗʰ in the melody, called the *Kenny Barron Chord.* However, playing it on the first bar would make it sound too low on your piano, so stacked 3rds is the better choice.

Now look at the second bar of Bars 1-4, a G7alt chord with the root in the melody. Again, look at The Menu. Do you see a dominant chord with root designated just to its right? There are two choices: one on the fourth bar of the third line, *Fourth Chords,* shows a G7 *chord with the root* in the melody. There is another voicing for a G7alt chord with the root in the melody, the very last one on the last line, called (my term) the *everything chord.*[19] We'll choose this one, because although it has only one more note than the one from the *fourth chords,* it has a fuller, richer sound.

Look at the third bar of Bars 1-4, a C major chord with the 3ʳᵈ in the melody. See a two-handed voicing for this on The Menu? There isn't one, so look up at the first line of the Menu, *left-hand voicings.* There are two voicings for a major chord on the top line of The Menu, *left-hand Voicings.* These are also called *rootless voicings,* because the bottom note in each is not the root of the chord. Again, the little numbers shown to the right of each melody note show their positions in the chord. None of them has the 3ʳᵈ in the melody, so a *left-hand voicing* will do.

---

19 Because it contains all seven notes of the altered scale.

A word about left-hand voicings.[20] You should memorize the two sets shown, each played on a II-V-I in the key of C, in all twelve keys as soon as possible, as II-V-I is the most played chord progression found in jazz.

Now look at the fourth bar of *Bars 1-4*, a major 7th chord with the 9th in the melody. There is one, in the 4th bar of line 2, the *So What chords*. Playing it on this chord would put it too low on your piano, so a *left-hand voicing* again works best. If the chord sounds too harsh to you, simply omit the bottom E to create a root-position chord.

Now look at **Bars 1-4a,** for the first four bars harmonized. Play them and listen to the sounds. Left-hand voicings mix well with any two-handed voicing. When you switch from four notes to as many as six from chord to chord, they still flow smoothly.

BARS 1-4A

Now look at Bars 5-8. The first melody note in the first bar, "D" is the 5th of a G7 chord. Looking at The Menu, this corresponds to the chord in the fourth bar of *fourth chords*. In the second bar of Bars 5-8, we see "E," the root in the melody of an E7alt chord. Look down The Menu and see if you can find an "alt" chord with the root in the melody. Yes, there is one on the *Upper Structures* line, in the second bar.

BARS 5-8

The example on The Menu is based on a C7alt chord, but the "alt" chord in Alice is an E7alt chord, so you'll have to transpose. Look at the Roman numeral beneath the chord – "bVI."

---

20 Practice them in all keys.

That number measures the distance between the root of the C7 chord up to the root of the Ab major triad. An "alt" chord requires a bVI upper structure. Back to the second bar a b6 above E would be C, and a C major triad would sit on top of the 3rd and 7th (Ab and D)[21] of the E7alt chord.

In the third bar of *Bars 5-8* is an A-7 chord with E the 5th in the melody. Looking at The Menu, you can spot that in the first bar of the *So What Chords*. In the fourth bar of Bars 5-8, the melody is a G, the 3rd of an Eb7 chord. There isn't a good two-hand example in The Menu so a *left-hand voicing* is your best choice.

Bars 5-8a shows the harmonization of *Bars 5-8*.

BARS 5-8A

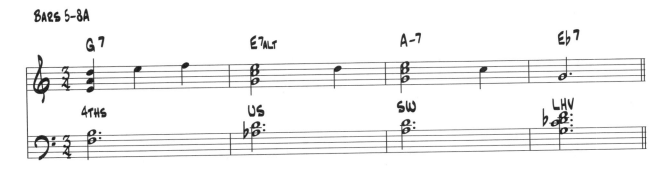

Now, look at **Bars 9-12.** Bar 9 has a G7 with the 5th in the melody. Again, look in The Menu for a dominant chord with the 5th in the melody. You'll find it in the fourth bar of the *Fourth Chords*.

Bar 10 has a richer chord, a G7b9 with a +4 as well.[22] Look at the *Upper Structures* line and you'll see that chord in the last bar, a C7b9 also with a +4. With a different root (G instead of C), you will have to transpose the voicing shown in The Menu so it will work for the G7b9 +4 chord. This is a big six-note chord that I have heard Herbie Hancock play. Hear how the melody note (E) is doubled for a richer sonority.

---

21 The G# is shown in Bars 5-8a as an Ab.

22 +4 and +11 are the same note – just different ways of notating the same thing. The 6th and 13th are also the same note, but by tradition, 6th is used on a major or minor chord, 13th on a dominant chord.

The third bar in **Bars 9-12** shows a C major chord with the 3rd in the melody. This is the same chord and melody found in the third bar of the song, and should be voiced the same way, with a *left-hand voicing*.

Bar 12 shows an A7alt chord, which suggests that you play the alt voicing shown in the *Upper Structures* line of The Menu. The melody is so high that you will need to double the melody .

Bars 9-12a shows the harmonization of **Bars 9-12**.

BARS 9-12A

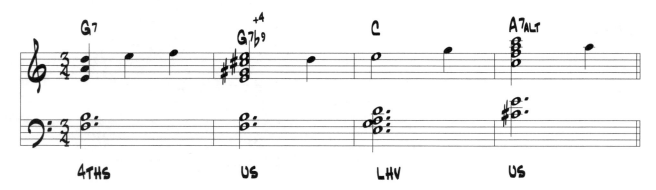

Now look at **Bars 13-16**. Bar 13 is a minor 7th chord with the 4th in the melody, which suggests either a *stacked 3rds* or a *Kenny Barron chord*. Because the melody is so high, the *Kenny Barron Chord* will sound best.

BARS 13-16

Bar 14 shows a Gsus chord with the 13th in the melody. There is a voicing in the *fourth chords* line that fits this chord perfectly.

Bar 15, the first bar in the first ending, has a Bb7+4 chord with the 13th in the melody. Dominant chords with any alteration suggest an *Upper Structures Chord:* the one with the Roman numeral "II" under it is the perfect solution.

Bar 16 in Bars 13-16, just before the repeat sign, shows an Eb7 chord with the 3rd in the melody, the same situation as in bar #8 of "Alice," although an octave higher, which doesn't change anything when playing *left-hand voicings.*

Bars 13-16a shows the voicings for these four bars.

BARS 13-16A

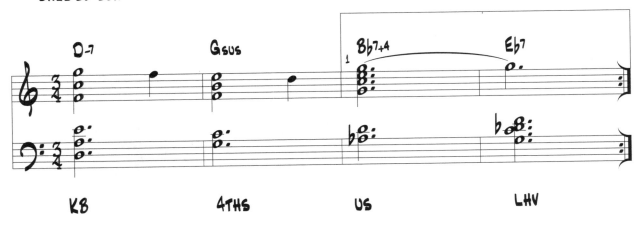

We have now completed the first 16 bars of the song. I bet by now you have "memorized" (I prefer the term *internalized*) some of the voicings. If so, you are well on your way to being able to do this without referring so often to The Menu.

Bars 17-20 start with the second ending, the first bar of which is a C major chord with the root in the melody, which is the same chord as in the first bar of the *Fourth Chords.*

BARS 17-20

The second bar in Bars 17-20 shows an A7alt chord with a +9 in the melody. Remember, dominant chords with any alteration suggest an *upper structure chord,* and an "alt" chord would be the *upper structure chord* bVI because it contains a #9.

The chord right before rehearsal letter B is an A7b9 chord with a C# in the melody, *Upper Structure* VI.

The first chord at rehearsal letter B is a D7 chord with the root in the melody. This immediately suggests a *Fourth Chord*. However, the spread of the chord goes just a bit too low[23], so a *left-hand voicing* is indicated.

The last bar in *Bars 17-20* has a Gsus chord with the 9th in the melody. This voicing appears in the last bar of the *fourth chords*.

Bars 17-20a shows the voicings for *Bars 17-20*.

Bars 17-20a

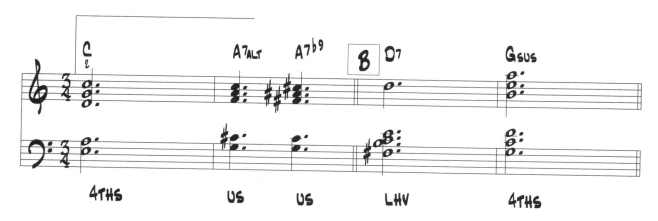

Bars 21-24 (on the following page) show an E7alt chord in the first bar with G, the +9, in the melody. We've had a few alt chords so far, and hopefully you remember that it calls for an *upper structure* chord. Which one? If you don't remember, it's bVI. That would mean the 3rd and 7th of the chord, Ab[24] and D, in the left hand, with a triad a minor 6th above E, the root. In other words, a C major triad.

The second bar of Bars 21-24 is an A-7 chord with C, the 3rd in the melody. Again, this is not the first example of a minor 7th chord with the 3rd in the melody, so you hopefully remember that it calls for a *left-hand voicing*.
The third bar of Bars 21-24 has a D-7 chord with the root in the melody, again not the first time in "Alice." By now you should start to remember which of the voicings will

---

23 A chord that sounds either too low (muddy) or too high (like a tinny-sounding music box) is subject to the limitations of your piano. If you have a 9' concert grand, the *fourth chord* mentioned might sound OK. On the other hand, if you have a 90-year old upright piano found in an old practice room at your school, even this chord can sound too high to be comfortable. If you're playing a keyboard, which has no overtones, all bets are off!. On any piano you have to establish your own parameters on what sounds too low or too high.
24 G# and Ab are *enharmonic,* meaning the same note spelled two different ways. Ab is the same note as G#.

BARS 21-24

work well, so you will have less need to consult The Menu. Repetition breeds familiarity! It calls for a *left-hand voicing.*

The last bar has a G7 chord with the melody note G. That's going to be a *fourth chord,* a simpler choice than the *everything chord.*

Bars 21-24a shows the harmonization of these four measures.

BARS 21-24A

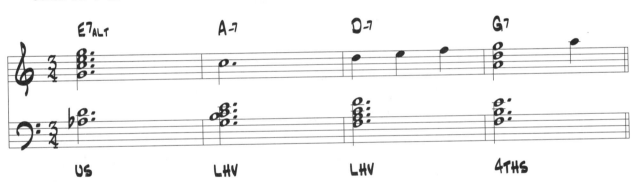

Bars 25-28 shows an E-7 chord with the 5th in the melody, calling for a *So What chord.* This is followed by an F major chord in the second bar with the 7th in the melody, also calling for a *So What chord.* This an interesting situation, an example of *parallelism,* where two identical chords follow one an another, but in a different place on the piano, often with different functions.

The third bar in *Bars 25-28* has a D7 chord with the 3rd in the melody. This again calls for a *left-hand voicing.*

BARS 25-28

The last bar in *Bars 25-28* shows an F7 chord with the 5th in the melody, an obvious candidate for a *Fourth Chord*.

Bars 25-28a shows the harmonization of *Bars 25-28*.

BARS 25-28A

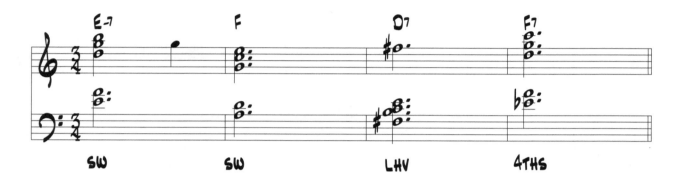

Bars 29-34 are the last six bars of the bridge of "Alice" before the D.C. al fine. Bar 29 has an E-7 chord with the 5th in the melody – a *So What chord* voicing. The next bar has an A7 chord with the 5th in the melody – a *Fourth Chord*. The third bar consists of a D-7 with the 5th in the melody – a *So What chord*. Am I going too fast? These last three chords already occurred so many times that I'm hoping you have them internalized by now.
The fourth bar has a Bb7 chord with the 5th in the melody – a *Fourth Chord*. The next-to-last chord in *Bars 29-34* shows an Ab7+4 chord – an *upper structure chord*. The last bar has a G7b9 chord with the 3rd in the melody – another *upper Structure Chord*.

BARS 29-34

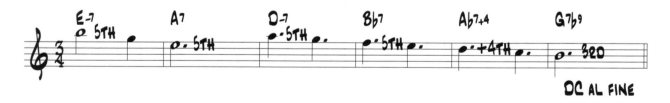

I zoomed through the last few bars very rapidly, in the hope that you could quickly guess the correct voicing. If you couldn't keep up, go back over each one, comparing the melody note with the chord in order to pick the best voicing.

Bars 29-34a shows the complete harmonization of the final six bars of Alice In Wonderland. Remember, the voicings shown in The Menu are only a partial list of choices. Many more can be found in my *Jazz Piano Book,*[25] other books, and most importantly, you can find

them with your ears when you *transcribe.*

PRACTICE TIPS

If you have classical training, what piece do you know from memory? Close the fall board on your piano. What is the first note of that piece (or lowest note if it's a chord) in your left hand? No, don't wiggle your fingers! Ah, its an A. What's the next note? And the next? And the next one? Most people hit a wall very quickly. I thought you knew this piece? So what part of your brain remembers what to play? Its *your fingers. Muscle memory,* finger memory, tactile memory - whatever you want to call it is how we learn. It also helps that the piano is a *color-coded instrument.* The notes are either black or white. A C#7alt chord has six white notes but only one black note.[26]

Use this knowledge when you practice! When you are practicing the Kenny Barron chord around the cycle of 5ths, aim your right hand little finger toward the 4th of the chord, and your left hand little finger toward the root. Stretch your fingers so that each hand plays two perfect 5ths. Keep a half-step between your thumbs. Now *without wiggling your fingers,* move to the next chord in the cycle of 5ths.[27]

---

25 Sher Music Co.
26 By contrast, all the notes of a C#7alt chord on a trumpet of trombone are brass-colored, all bass and guitar notes are string-colored, and so forth.
27 An arrangement of all 12 notes in the chromatic scale going down in 5ths, in a counterclockwise direction. Classical musicians go clockwise, which is of no use when improvising. The roots of the II-V-I in C are D, G and C, the notes moving counterclockwise. The roots of the first five chords in the standard "All The Things You Are" are F, Bb, Eb, Ab and Db – five chords in a row moving counterclockwise.

Repeat this method when learning how to play all chords – *So What, Fourth Chords, Upper Structures,* and more.

Have fun, and *practice!*

FIGURE 1-7 shows the entire "Alice in Wonderland" voiced from The Menu.

FIGURE 1-7 · ALICE IN WONDERLAND · MUSIC BY SAMMY FAIN · LYRIC BY BOB HILLIARD

Mark Levine

chapter two: applying the menu

FIGURE 2-1 shows a lead sheet to Harry Warren's[1] classic song "You're My Everything."

Figure 2-1

YOU'RE MY EVERYTHING

HARRY WARREN

---

1   Joe Young is listed as a co-composer, with lyrics by Mort Dixon.

The chord changes are quite different from the original, mostly adapted from Freddie Hubbard's CD "Hub-Tones,"[2] but simplified both rhythmically and harmonically for this book. I'll introduce some new voicings, even a couple in *root position*.

After voicing 'Alice,' you probably know most of the ways to voice a song from *The Menu,* so I'm going to give you far fewer hints this time around.

Short test:

What are the two voicings I suggested that you use for a minor seventh chord with the 4th in the melody?

What is the best voicing to use for a dominant seventh chord with the 3rd in the melody? If you can't answer correctly, I hereby give you permission to look back at The Menu in Chapter One!

What is the best voicing to use for C7b9? for C7+4? For C7alt?

Look at **Figure 2-2**, 'Alice' again, with just the melody notes indicated. How accurately can you play it?

---

2   Freddie Hubbard, *Hub-Tones,* Blue Note, 1962.

Figure 2-2

Alice In Wonderland
Sammy Fain & Bob Hilliard

Look at **Figure 2-3**, 'Alice' one more time, this time with the chord types shown. How accurately can you play it?

FIGURE 2-3
PIANO

ALICE IN WONDERLAND

Now go all the way back to the lead sheet for 'Alice,' **Figure 1-1**. How accurately can you play it?

OK, let's go on to "You're My Everything"!

"You're My Everything" is shown in full with voicings at the end of this chapter as Figure 2-14.

Look at **Bars 1-4**, the first four bars of "You're My Everything."[3] Something new has been added: a bass clef without notes or rests. That's right – you're going to have to fill them in yourself. And use a pencil, not a pen. If you don't have all the voicings with their melody notes internalized, go back to The Menu in Chapter One and review them.

BARS 1-4

Look at the first (pickup) bar, with E in the melody over a G7b9 chord. E is how much above G, the root of the chord? I'm not going to tell you this time! If you have trouble identifying intervals, here's a primer on how to do it: **Figure 2-4**, titled *intervals*.[4]

An *interval* is the space between two notes. **Figure 2-4** shows each interval, from a half-step to an octave. Note the alternate name (shown above) for the minor sixth. Both names shown above the C and Db, and the C and D are used about equally.

---

3 The pickup bar is not numbered, and from here on in the text, I'll call the song "Everything."
4 I'm going to be inserting a lot of theory into Chapter Two of this book. Even if you've studied the theory in *The Jazz Piano Book* or *The Jazz Theory Book,* read these insertions because they contain new material.

FIGURE 2-4

INTERVALS

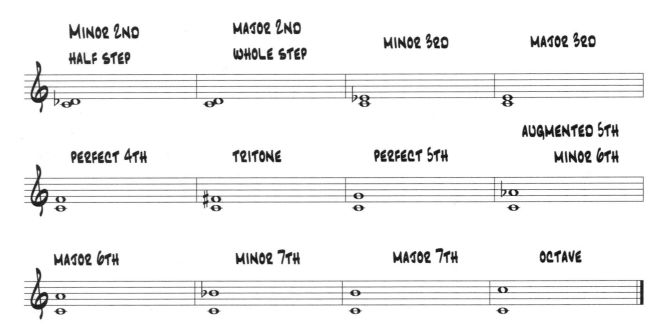

Inverting intervals: major becomes minor / minor becomes major / perfect remains perfect / tritone remains tritone / and the two intervals add up to "9"

Play the intervals on your piano, based on C. Then do so without looking at the music, and with your eyes closed. Listen to what each interval sounds like. There are certain clichés, for example that a minor interval sounds sadder than the major interval with the same number (as in a minor 3rd sounds sadder than a major 3rd). It also helps to connect intervals to their use in tunes. For instance, the first two notes in "Over The Rainbow" form an octave. The second and third notes in Cole Porter's "I Love You" form a descending major 7th.

Look at the text lines at the bottom of **Figure 2-4**, called *inverting intervals*. This is important for several reasons, not the least of which is having to transpose while accompanying singers, who may ask you to play "Lush Life," normally in the key of Db, in the key of B. Yikes! It's much easier to transpose down a major 2nd (from Db *down* to B) than up a minor 7th (From Db *up* to B).

Look at *inverting intervals* again:
• A major interval becomes a minor interval when
    inverted, as in a major 3rd becomes a minor 6th
• A minor interval becomes a major interval when
    inverted, as in a minor 7th becomes a major 2nd.
I'll let you work out the rest yourself, but note that *the two intervals add up to 9.* Wow, the Nobel prize in Music should have gone to whoever noticed that first!

Now repeat the process based on F, then Bb, then Eb, then Ab, and so on, around the *cycle of 5ths,* which was shown back in **Figure 1-2**.

Return to **Bars 1-4** of "Everything," the G-7 in the second bar, with an E, the 6th, in the melody. I don't think there was an example of this in 'Alice.' Look down The Menu (I know I just told you to try not to look back at it, but I will grant you a temporary dispensation), and tell me if you see a minor 7th chord with the 6th [5] notated anywhere. There isn't one, so use a *left-hand voicing.* **Bars 1-4** should be easy as both bars feature II-V progressions, which suggest…you should know by now!

Bars 5-8 start with a minor seventh chord with the 4th in the melody – you have two choices, one with the notes close together, the other with the notes spread wide apart. Let your ears decided which one to use. The third bar of **Bars 5-8** has a G7 chord with the 13th in the melody. Do you remember this from The Menu? The top note of the G7 voicing is E, the same note as the melody. Rather than use two fingers to play the same note an octave apart, omit the E in the left hand.

BARS 5-8

---

5   The 6th and 13th are the same note. *On minor and major chords, it is notated as "6th". On dominant chords, it is notated as "13th."*

The fourth bar in **Bars 5-8** has a new chord: F-+7, called *F minor-major* because it has a minor 3rd and a major 7th. It is similar to an F-7 chord, except that the 7th has been raised. **Figure 2-5** shows the chord first in root position, then as a *left-hand voicing.* Left-hand voicings usually have the 3rd or the 7th as the bottom note. However, the melody here is very low, which would force a left-hand voicing into the muddy range, so I've rearranged the notes with the 7th on the bottom. This voicing is one that you won't hear in your supermarket or hotel elevator! Play it both ways to hear what it sounds like. This chord is from the *melodic minor scale. Melodic minor* scales and chords come from the folk music of Eastern Europe.

FIGURE 2-5

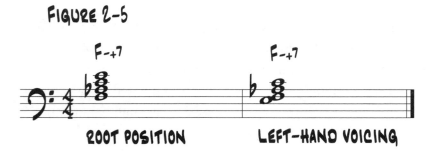

ROOT POSITION   LEFT-HAND VOICING

What's the big deal – Western Europe? Eastern Europe? they're both Europe. Well, back in the seventeenth and eighteenth centuries, if you wanted to go from Paris to Budapest, it took you a couple of weeks by stage coach and you might get held up and robbed 2-3 times. There was no internet, no airmail, no telephones at the time, so the influence of one composer took a while to influence another composer 500 miles away.

The melodic minor scale is a very different animal than the Western European major scale of Bach, Beethoven, and Duke Ellington. Ah, but changing even one note changes almost everything, especially the relationships between the notes, and the resulting chords. That one change, with a *minor 3rd* replacing the major 3rd in the scale, gives it and its resulting chords a darker sound than the major scale and its chords.

Take a look at **Figure 2-6**, which shows a comparison between the C major and C melodic minor scales. The major scale has only one tritone, between the 4th and 7th of the scale (**Figure 2-6,** top treble clef). The *melodic minor scale* has two tritones, between the 3rd and 6th of the scale, as well as between the 4th and 7th (**Figure 2-6**, bottom treble clef).

FIGURE 2-6

MAJOR SCALE TRITONE   TRITONE..

MELODIC MINOR SCALE TRITONES   TRITONE..

TRITONE...

There are also melodic minor *key signatures*, found rarely in Western classical music.[6] The key signature for the above C *melodic minor* scale would be one flat, but the flat *would be Eb*. The key signature for F-Δ, the last chord in **Bars 5-8** would be two flats, but the flats would be Ab and Bb. What? Is that a major scale key signature?

Although I said that these key signatures are seldom found in Western music, *this is what you see on the piano when you play a chord in a melodic minor key*. This is called a *visual aspect*. It's the way pianists *see* when they play[7] black notes and white notes. The piano is a *color-coordinated* instrument. If you're playing the trumpet, the only color you see is brass. If you're playing a C#7alt chord (don't ask, we're not there yet), you will *see* and *play* six white notes and one black note (C#), and you're in the *key* of D melodic minor. You're not in Kansas any more![8] There is more on the melodic minor scale in **Appendix I**.

6 Béla Bartók, *The Mikrokosmos,* Boosey & Hawkes.
7 Can you guess what other instrument is color-coordinated? It's the harp.
8 For my non-Western readers, "You're not in Kansas anymore" comes from the popular classic movie *The Wizard of Oz,* in which the world appears to be upside down.

Now look at **Bars 9-12**. Bar 9 has E-7, a minor seventh chord with the 3rd in the melody. Do you remember a voicing from The Menu for that?

BARS 9-12

The second bar of **Bars 9-12** has an Eb-7 chord with the 5th in melody. Remember that one from The Menu?

The third bar of **Bars 9-12** has an old familiar minor 7th chord with the 5th in the melody.

The final bar of **Bars 9-12** has a brand new chord, a *half-diminished* chord[9]. The use of the word *diminished* is unfortunate because it implies that it is somehow related to the *diminished* chord. There is a slight connection, but its more like thinking of someone from North Carolina as being from *Carolina*, leaving out the *North.*

The *half-diminished chord symbol* is shorthand for a *minor seventh chord with a flatted 5th*. That's a mouthful, and takes up too much space on the page. Many chord symbols have abbreviated shorthand symbols, and this is one of them. The ø symbol represents the Greek letter *phi*.

Let's use a root-position chord on this ø chord. The best one is from a chord type called *three-note voicings*. They are the subject of Chapter Three in this book, so more on them later. For now, on a three-note voicing, play the root in the left hand and the 3rd and 7th in the right hand, with the melody note added on top.

The ø chord is also from *melodic minor* harmony. Here is a very short primer on melodic minor harmony:
The 3rd and 7th of dominant seventh chords in the melodic minor scale do not have the same importance as they do on the dominant seventh chords from the major scale.

_____

9   Shorthand is common for the half-diminished chord symbol: ø

The most characteristic notes in any melodic minor chord are the 3rd, 5th, 7th, and 9th of the melodic minor *key, not the chord.* Because Bø is from the *key* of D melodic minor, the important notes are F, A, C# and E, the 3rd, 5th, 7th and 9th of D melodic minor, as shown in **Figure 2-7**. This may seem strange to you at first, but please go to **Appendix I**, for more information

FIGURE 2-7

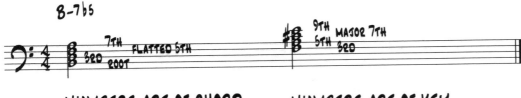

NUMBERS ARE OF CHORD

NUMBERS ARE OF KEY OF D MELODIC MINOR

You can arrange any 4-note *left-hand voicing* and play them in any inversion. **Figure 2-8** shows the ø voicing in all four inversions. To my ears, the first and third are the most pleasing. If you're not used to hearing them yet, listen to some Herbie Hancock records!

FIGURE 2-8

NUMBERS OF BOTTOM NOTES (F, A, C#, E) ARE THEIR POSITION IN THE KEY OF D MELODIC MINOR, NOT THE CHORD!

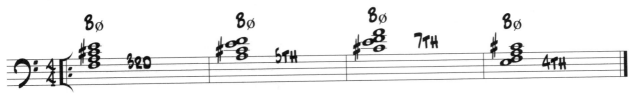

If they are still not pleasing, you can use the Bill Evans root position version of the ø chord, as shown in **Figure 2-9.**

FIGURE 2-9

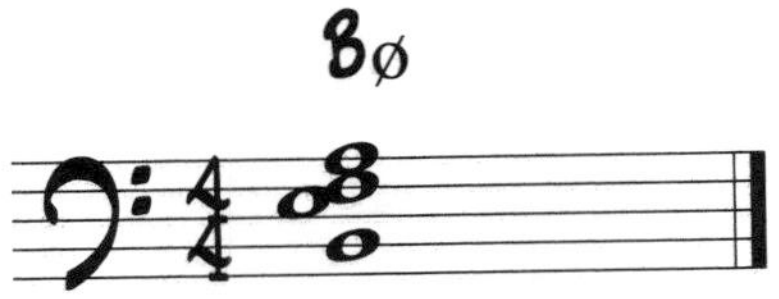

Remember, the important notes in any chord from the melodic minor scale and its resultant chords are notes *from the key, not the chord.* More, much more, on this in **Appendix I**.

The last chord in **Bars 9-12** is an E7b9 chord. Recognize it? There was one example in 'Alice.' The top note of the voicing is the same as the melody note, so you can omit it in the left hand.

BARS 13-16

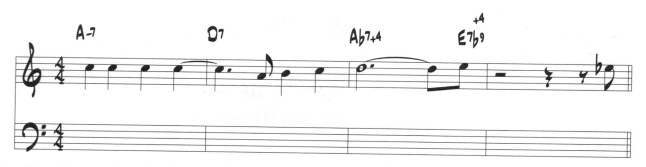

The first and second bars of **Bars 13-16** start out with the an A-7 chord with the 3rd in the melody, which resolves to D7. What voicings usually work best in II-V progressions?

The third bar of **Bars 13-16** shows an Ab7+4 chord. That suggests an *upper structure* voicing. Which one had a +4? No, I ain't gonna tell you! That bar ends with a very brief explosion, an E7b9+4 chord. Do you remember that Herbie Hancock chord? It often helps to remember a voicing if it's associated with a particular pianist. The rhythm section usually stops on this chord, with a break, and comes back in, in the first bar of **Bars 17-20**.

BARS 17-20

Bars 17-20 start out like Bar 1 of the song. For variety's sake, however, I've suggested the second of the two voicings shown in The Menu used on minor seventh chords with the 4th in the melody as it modulates to a Gb7+4 chord with the 13th in the melody in the second bar of **Bars 17-20**. I've opted to use a *root-position* voicing here. The voicing is shown in **Figure 2-10**. Modern pianists mix rootless voicings with root-position voicings all the time.[10]

FIGURE 2-10

The third bar of **Bars 17-20** shows an F7+4 chord, an obvious *upper structure* choice. The final bar in **Bars 17-20** starts with an E-7 chord with the 5th in the melody. If you haven't got this one memorized by now, Do Not Pass Go, Do Not Collect $200![11]

The second chord in the last bar of **Bars 17-20** shows an A7b9 chord with the root in the melody. What is your choice?

Bars 21-24 start with a D-7 chord with G, the 4th in the melody. At this point, let me introduce a new type of voicing to you called *Drop2*. First, a bit of theory:

BARS 21-24

---

10 Listen to solo recordings by Mulgrew Miller for good examples of this approach
11 From the popular board game *Monopoly*.

Chord tones are the root, 3rd, 5th and 7th of a chord (C, E, G, and B on a C major 7th chord). They define whether the chord is major, minor, or dominant. *Passing tones,* on the other hand, are the filler notes in between: the 2nd, 4th and 6th notes in the scale that go with the chord (D, F and A on a C major seventh chord). Got that? You will need to know this if you want to play *Drop2.* That 4th (G) in the D-7 chord is called a *passing tone.*

One beat later, the melody drops a whole-step, and is now F, a *chord tone*. This sets up the chance to use *drop 2*. You voice the melody note G as a diminished chord, see **Figure 2-11**, but to make it more pianistic, you take the second note from the top of the chord and *drop it an octave,* as shown in **Figure 2-12.** See more, much more, on *drop2* in **Appendix 2.**[12]

FIGURE 2-11

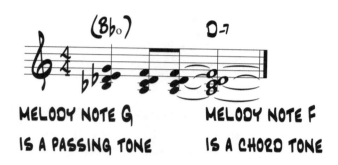

MELODY NOTE G IS A PASSING TONE

MELODY NOTE F IS A CHORD TONE

FIGURE 2-12

The two last chords in **Bars 21-24** are a Bø chord followed by an E7b9+4 chord. This is called a *minor II-V* [13]. The Bø chord, derived from D melodic minor, is voiced with the essential notes from D melodic minor, the 3rd, 5th, 7th and 9th of the *key,* not the *chord.*

---

12 Much, much more on *drop2* voicings in my book *The Drop2 Book* (Sher Music).
13 Bø followed by an E7alt chord is another version of a *minor II-V.*

Because the top note of the chord is the same as in the melody, you omit the top note.

The E7b9+4 chord is voiced, not as the *upper structure* chord from The Menu, but as a *left-hand voicing*. Simply play the left-hand voicing for Bø but lower the 7th a half-step as you would in a normal II-V progression. Again, the top note of the voicing in the left hand duplicates the melody, so you can omit it.

BARS 25-28

Bars 25-28 start with an A minor 7th chord with the 3rd in the melody, then goes down a half step to an Ab7 chord with the 3rd in the melody, then a G-7 chord with the 5th in the melody. These chromatically descending bass note chords against a largely static melody create a rich patina of colors using the voicings that you have learned so far.

The G-7 chord in the second bar of **Bars 25-28** is a simple choice. But the next chord, a C7+5 with the 9th in the melody, is a new type of chord. A dominant seventh chord with a +5 usually indicates a chord derived from the *whole-tone scale*.[14] I've used a *drop2* voicing in the second bar of **Bars 25-28**, followed by the melody notes C, A, and F, which outline an F6 chord. Because these are all *chord tones,* I've continued the use of *drop 2* here.

The Bb7+4 chord in the last bar of **Bars 25-28** calls for an *upper structure* voicing. Can you remember which one to use?

---

14 The *whole-tone scale* is one of two artificial scales used in jazz, the other being the *diminished scale.* They are called artificial scales because, unlike the major and melodic minor scales, they are not derived from folk music.

Mark Levine, Chuck Sher, Michael Aragon and Gene Perla

Bars 29-32 bring "You're My Everything" to a close. An E-7 chord with the 3rd in the melody brings to mind – do you remember? The following chord, Eb-7 with the 4th in the melody should be firmly imprinted in your brain by now, as well as the D-7 chord with the 5th in the melody. The G7b9 chord suggests which *upper structure* voicing?

BARS 29-32

The final chord, Ab7 is perhaps the most surprising of the song. The logical final chord should be a C chord, but Ab7 substitutes for it, and lasts two bars, allowing the soloist to stretch out a bit.

The complete version of "You're My Everything" is shown in **Figure 2-13.**

FIGURE 2-13

YOU'RE MY EVERYTHING

HARRY WARREN

And now on to a much simpler way to voice standards:
Minimalism.

Mark Levine

chapter three: minimalism ~ beatrice

Is your head still spinning from learning how to use all the new voicings? If so, this chapter will soothe your brain, as we introduce *three-note voicings,* consisting of the root in the left hand, and the 3rd and 7th in the right hand. These voicings represent the differences between major, minor, and dominant chords, the essence of Western harmony.[1]

• The major seventh chord has a major 3rd and a major 7th
• The minor seventh chord has a minor 3rd and a minor 7th
• The dominant seventh chord has a major 3rd and a minor 7th

I call this approach *minimalism,* because it reduces the essential harmony of a song to just three notes, plus the melody note, which is often the 3rd or the 7th, eliminating the need for a fourth note.

Figure 3-1 shows a lead sheet to Sam Rivers' piece "Beatrice," only 16 bars long, but long a favorite among jazz musicians.[2] There is more music packed into these 16 bars than in most tunes that jazz musicians love to play, with the switch from major to minor tonality in the next-to-last bar, the deceptive "hook" to the song.

---

1 Western harmony is different than *melodic minor, diminished and whole-tone harmony,* which use some of the same rules, but not exclusively.
2 Sam Rivers, *Fuchsia Swing Song,* Blue Note Records; Joe Henderson, *The Art of the Tenor,* Blue Note Records.

FIGURE 3-1

BEATRICE

SAM RIVERS

First, let's learn *three-note voicings*. **Figure 3-2** shows how this works. In the bass clef of both bars are the roots of the II-V-I chords in the key of C: D, G and C. *II-V-I* is the most common chord progression played in jazz. Notice the motion in the bass from D-7: first down, then up. The opposite (first up, then down) works just as well, but in either case, make sure you play bass notes no higher than the G below middle C. You can easily play bass notes an octave below where they are written, as long as your ear can distinguish the notes.

On **Figure 3-2**, you move your left hand bass note from D to G. In the right hand, C, the 7th of the D-7 chord moves down a half-step becoming B, the 3rd of G7. F, the 3rd of the D-7 chord stays the same.

FIGURE 3-2

3-NOTE VOICINGS

LEFT HAND PLAYS THE ROOT
RIGHT HAND PLAYS THE 3RD & 7TH
7TH ALWAYS COMES DOWN A HALF-STEP
WHEN GOING FROM II TO V, AND V TO I

Then, to get from G7 to C, your left hand plays the bass note C and in your right hand you lower the 7th (now an F) down a half-step to E. You have now played all the *essential notes* in the *II-V-I* chords.

In the second bar of **Figure 3-2** the right hand notes are reversed, the 3rd above the 7th on the D-7 chord. Everything else follows the same pattern as in the first bar. The 7th of each chord comes down a half-step when going to the following chord.

To sum up:
• The left hand plays the root.
• The right hand plays the 3rd and 7th (or 7th and 3rd).
• The 7th always comes down a half-step, when going from
     II to V, and from V to I.

These voicings are also great when you're learning how to 'comp,' as they provide the three essential notes (root, 3rd, and 7th) of almost all chords. For now, you don't have to worry about playing any b9s, +9s, +4s, b13s, and getting in anyone's way. And ignore the old saying about "getting in the way of the bass player" when playing roots. That should have been retired decades ago.

Before you go any further, practice the progression in the *first bar* around the cycle of 5ths,[3] until you can play it easily and flawlessly. Now do the same with the progression in the *second bar* until you achieve the same proficiency.

Look at **Figure 3-3**, a blank chord work sheet that you can use to work from. Just fill in the root (in the bass clef), and the 3rd and 7th (in the treble clef).

FIGURE 3-3
CHORD WORK SHEET

_____

3   The *cycle of 5ths* was explained in the diagram on page 5 in Chapter One.

Look at the first bar of Beatrice in **Figure 3-3**, an F major 7th chord.[4] Play the root with your left hand, and the 3rd and 7th, or 7th and 3rd. it makes no difference at this point, but pick one or the other.

Then in the second bar, move your right hand to the *closest* 3rd and 7th of the Gb+4[5] chord. Don't worry about the +4, as you're just playing root, 3rd and 7th at this point. Continue through the tune, always going to the *closest* 3rd and 7th of the next chord. **Figure 3-4** shows the first four bars of "Beatrice" starting with the 3rd on top.

FIGURE 3-4

Figure 3-5 shows the first four bars starting with the 7th on top.

FIGURE 3-5

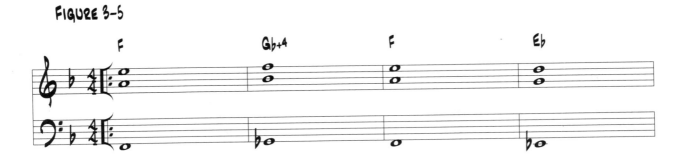

Remember, play the above examples with no melody. Continue through the tune this way until you've completed the song.

---

4   Many musicians notate this chord as FΔ, the Δ meaning "major 7th."
5   Many musicians notate this chord as GbΔ+4.

When you reach the end of the song, it *might* (depending on which way you started, with either the 3rd or the 7th on top) look like **Figure 3-6**. There is one bar with two chords in it (E-7 and A7 in the third line), and in that bar use a half note for each chord.

FIGURE 3-6

Chords tend to go *left* on the piano, as progressions resolve downwards. If you think that you're starting to get too low, flip the notes over, reversing the position of the 3rd and 7th, as shown in **Figure 3-7**.

FIGURE 3-7

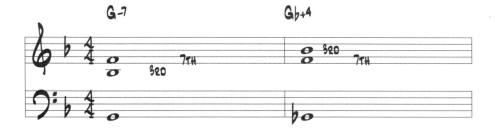

Now it's time to add the melody. Look at **Figure 3-8**, a lead sheet with the stems all pointed up, and the bass clef left blank. This will be your work sheet as you fill in the root, 3rd and 7th.

On many chords, the melody will already be the 3rd or 7th. If so, you won't need to add an extra note. This happens first in the second bar, where the melody note on the Gb+4 chord is F, the 7th. Just make sure that you keep the melody on top.

FIGURE 3-8   BEATRICE   SAM RIVERS

WORK SHEET

Continue this way until you reach the end of the tune. The complete version is shown as **Figure 3-9**.

FIGURE 3-9   BEATRICE   SAM RIVERS

You will notice that a couple of the chords are anticipated in the bass (last three bars). It's always good to do this when the melody anticipates over a bar line.

Congratulations! Now get out your fake book[6] and start.
(And don't forget to practice!)

---

6 Most Fake Books are shamefully inaccurate, the original *Real Book* and the *Vocal Real Book* being the worst examples. Stick to the proven ones that most jazz musicians use, the Sher Music series and the lead sheets with the Jamey Aebersold play-along books.

Brian Bowman, Mark Levine, Greg D'augelli

ephemera Q&A

Q: I have trouble playing "bad notes" when I improvise.
A: You're never further away than a half-step from a "good note" on any chord. Simply raise or lower your "bad" note a half step to a "good" note. This is true of any chord and scale except the blues scale.

Q: I've heard that music is called a language.
A: Languages have alphabets. The English alphabet has 26 letters. Jazz theory is also a language. It has an alphabet of only 7 letters and 13 numbers.[1] Think about that for a minute. You can do it – rocket science it is not!

Q: Are fake books valuable?
A: When you read a tune in a fakebook you see a string of dots on the page and some chord symbols. And you might be able to sit down and play the tune and get an idea of what it sounds like. But on a recording of the same tune, you hear the melody line, you hear the inflections, you hear the phrasing, you hear the dynamics, the breathing, the emotions of the players, the interactions of all the players, all the drum stuff, all the bass stuff, all the piano voicings. In fact, you also hear the history of the music, each individual players' own history, their relationships with their wives, husbands, kids, parents, etc. It all comes through in the music.

There's all this stuff that you don't get from a printed page. You only get this when you listen.

Q: What's the most important elements in learning how to play jazz?
A: The most important elements are the things that you learn on the bandstand. That type of knowledge is so individual, so specific to the moment. It burns itself into your memory, especially if it's an exceptional good or exceptional bad experience. You never forget these things. It reshapes you day to day, gig to gig.

If a singer or a horn player turns around and says: "Four-bar intro," every time you do that, you learn something that works and something that doesn't work. Even if a teacher relates the experience that they had on their gig last night it's still gonna be a different experience than you have when you play tonight. I'm not talking about what the notes are in a D-7 chord. I'm talking about the creative process and the preparatory process that every musician has to go through to get to the point where you can actually play this music well.

---

1 A, B, C, D, E, F, and G.

Q: How can I prioritize what to practice?

A: Make a list of the things that you need to learn, like voicings, how to solo, repertoire, at least the changes, especially changes. If you work with singers you will need to learn how to transpose. If a pianist wants to work, work with singers. Furthermore to develop a solo style as well as a group style, to be as eclectic as possible, not to play everything with left-hand voicings for instance, but to be able to play root position, to play stride, block chords, bringing some variety not just to a set of tunes but to every single tune. This is the way Thelonious Monk practiced.

Q: How important is it to learn anything from other genres?

A: Learn as much about Latin music as possible. Salsa teaches you independent coordination of your hands. I teach my students to play montunos in their right hands, and then I have them play the bassline, the tumbao, in the left hand. They get a totally different conception of time. It's almost like turning time into a three dimensional subject, because they're taking the roles of two different people at the same time, and morphing it into a third person: the rhythm section. Then they can understand how a rhythm section functions.

And this carries over into jazz. It's interesting how many of the best piano players have some Latin roots. When Chick Corea first came to New York, he played with Willie Bobo. Herbie Hancock, when he came to New York, played with Mongo Santamaria. There's a polyrhythmic component to their music which you may not hear in other players that didn't have that experience.

appendix one: the melodic minor scale

The Melodic Minor scale is derived from the folk music of Eastern Europe. Béla Bartók famously used it as the source of many of the themes in his "Mikrokosmos."[1]

It is a scale that differs from the Western European Major scale in one way: it has a minor 3rd in place of the major 3rd of the music of Bach, Beethoven, and Duke Ellington. The resulting difference in the intervals between the notes creates a very different set of chords than the major scale and its chords.

There are a several important differences in the interval relationships between the major scale and the melodic minor scale:

• The major scale has a tritone between the 4th and 7th of the scale.
• The melodic minor scale has *two* tritones, between the 3rd and the 6th of the scale, and another, between the the 4th and 7th of the scale.

Both major and melodic minor scales with the position of their tritones are shown in **Figure A1-1**.

FIGURE A1-1

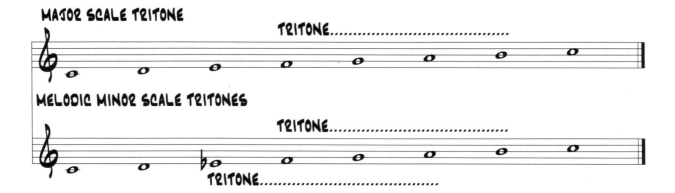

---

1   Béla Bartók, *The Mikrokosmos,* Boosey & Hawkes.

• The arrangement of diatonic 4ths is very different, as shown in **Figure A1-2**.
One of the diatonic 4ths (between B and Eb) is a *major 3rd*.

FIGURE A1-2

MAJOR SCALE FOURTHS

MELODIC MINOR SCALE FOURTHS

On the following page (**Figure A1-3**), you will see the C melodic minor scale, with all of its modes. Note the differences from major scale harmony:

1. In the first mode, there is a minor 3rd and a major 7th making it a *minor-major* chord.[2]

2. In the second mode, what appears to be a minor seventh chord with a flatted 9th (because it has a minor 3rd, a minor 7th, and a flatted 9th), actually functions as a *susb9 chord.*[3]

---

2   The first and second chords in Horace Silver's *Nica's Dream.* I have notated this chord as C-+7, but many musicians prefer to notate it as C-Δ.
3   The second chord on the first bar of the bridge in Horace Silver's *Nica's Dream.* Also the chords in the first, third, fifth and seventh bars of John Coltrane's *After The Rain.*

Figure A1-3

Melodic Minor Scale Harmony

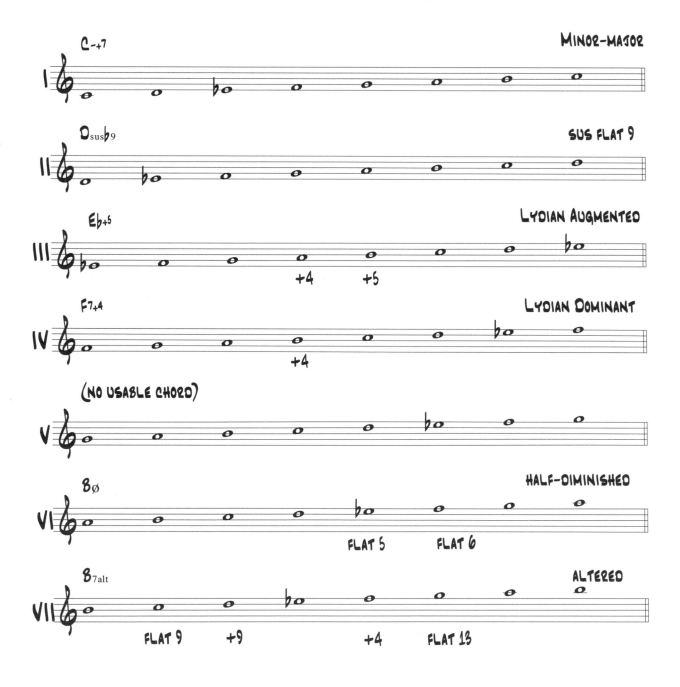

3. In the third mode, the scale has a major third and major seventh, making an Eb major seventh chord, but also has a sharp 4th and a sharp 5th, although only the +5 appears in the chord symbol. The chord symbol is Eb+5. The +4 is implied (and played) but omitted from the chord symbol.

4. In the fourth mode appears a more familiar F7+4 chord.

5. This chord is unusable, as it has both a natural 5th and a flatted 6th. One of those notes must be omitted for the chord to sound consonant.

6. This is the ø, or *half-diminished chord*,[4] replacing the older *Locrian mode* used in early bebop.

7. This is the *altered mode.* The fourth note in the scale functions as the *third* of the chord. The chord symbol is "alt," shorthand for *altered.*[5]

"You're not in Kansas anymore!"[6]
Western classical composers who occasionally used the *melodic minor scale* used it to *ascend* one way, and to *descend* another way, using the descending form exactly like (from the Western major scale) a descending *Aeolian Mode.*

---

4 The first chord in Dizzy Gillespie's *Woody 'n You.*
5 "altered" replaces the b9, +9, +4, and b13. Some musicians prefer b5 and +5 to +4 and b13, but I think its confusing enough to have a scale with not only two 9ths (b9 and +9°, and also a b5 and +a 5.
6 Nobody yet has analyzed the melodic minor on its own terms, rather than comparing "how it differs" from the major scale. The problem is complicated by the fact that major and melodic minor harmonies flow together smoothly. Most of the theory and usage was developed by jazz musicians living in New York in the late1940s and 1950s. Gil Evans, Hall Overton, and Miles Davis were among the creators.

The ascending *melodic minor scale*, shown in the top clef of **Figure A1-4**, is the same as the major scale except that it has a *minor 3rd*. The descending *melodic minor scale*, shown in the bottom clef of **Figure A1-4**, is the same as the Eb major scale starting on C, the *Aeolian mode* of the Eb major scale. Fortunately, jazz musicians just play the *ascending* form, whether or not we are *ascending* or *descending*.[7]

FIGURE A1-4

ASCENDING MELODIC MINOR SCALE

DESCENDING MELODIC MINOR SCALE (SAME AS AEOLIAN MODE OF E FLAT MAJOR)

7 Also check out the Chapter on Melodic Minor Harmony in both my *The Jazz Piano Book* and *The Jazz Theory Book.*

Mark Levine

appendix two: drop2

Drop2 is a voicing style derived from a way of writing for four saxes, trumpets, trombones, four anything, called *four-way close*, originally used as an arranging technique in the 1920s. It was first used as a piano technique in the early '40s, but although *four-way close* is still occasionally played, it uses too little of the piano to be considered "pianistic."[1]

Then, some unknown genius decided to take the second note from the top of the voicing and drop it an octave, and Drop2 was born. **Figure A2-1** shows how to get started, using a scale developed around the time that Charlie Parker arrived on the jazz scene, called *the bebop major scale.*[2]

As shown in **Figure A2-1** follow the instruction to play the scale with just your little finger, right hand.

FIGURE A2-1

THE C BEBOP MAJOR SCALE
PLAY WITH YOUR LITTLE FINGER, RIGHT HAND

---

1 George Shearing added one note, and improved the sound somewhat, although it's very saccharine, and is seldom played today. It is also related to Barber Shop Quartet Harmony.
2 There are other bebop scales as well, the most important being *the bebop dominant scale,* invented by John Phillip Sousa.

Figure A2-2 shows the bebop major scale harmonized, with just two chords: a C6 chord alternating with a diminished seventh chord. All the C6 chords are inversions of the same chord, and the same goes for all four diminished chords.

FIGURE A2-2

C BEBOP MAJOR SCALE IN FOUR-WAY CLOSE

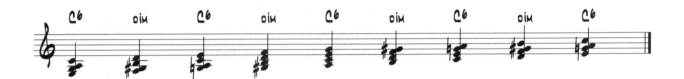

Figure A2-3 shows the bebop major scale with the second note from the top dropped an octave. Your ear will tell you that this version of the scale is much fuller, and more pianistic.

FIGURE A2-3

C BEBOP MAJOR SCALE IN DROP2

Figure A2-4 illustrates why the drop2 bebop major sounds so smooth. Each diminished chord is a *disguised V chord*, the V leading to the root of the following chord. As you can see, the addition of a bass part in the left hand reveals the chord progression to be just 1-V-1-V-1-V (C, G7, C, G7, C, G7, etc.).[3]

FIGURE A2-4

C AND G7 ALTERNATE - WHY DROP2 SOUNDS SO SMOOTH

----

3   For even more, much, much, much more on *drop2,* consult my book *Jazz Piano Masterclass: The Drop2 Book.*

SHER MUSIC CO. — *The finest in Jazz & Latin Publications*

THE NEW REAL BOOK SERIES

The Standards Real Book (C, Bb or Eb)

A Beautiful Friendship
A Time For Love
Ain't No Sunshine
Alice In Wonderland
All Of You
Alone Together
At Last
Baltimore Oriole
Bess, You Is My Woman
Bluesette
But Not For Me
Close Enough For Love
Crazy He Calls Me
Dancing In The Dark

Days Of Wine And Roses
Dreamsville
Easy To Love
Embraceable You
Falling In Love With Love
From This Moment On
Give Me The Simple Life
Have You Met Miss Jones?
Hey There
I Can't Get Started
I Concentrate On You
I Cover The Waterfront
I Love You
I Loves You Porgy

I Only Have Eyes For You
I'm A Fool To Want You
Indian Summer
It Ain't Necessarily So
It Never Entered My Mind
It's You Or No One
Just One Of Those Things
Love For Sale
Lover, Come Back To Me
The Man I Love
Mr. Lucky
My Funny Valentine
My Heart Stood Still
My Man's Gone Now

Old Folks
On A Clear Day
Our Love Is Here To Stay
'Round Midnight
Secret Love
September In The Rain
Serenade In Blue
Shiny Stockings
Since I Fell For You
So In Love
So Nice (Summer Samba)
Some Other Time
Stormy Weather
The Summer Knows

Summer Night
Summertime
Teach Me Tonight
That Sunday, That Summer
The Girl From Ipanema
Then I'll Be Tired Of You
There's No You
Time On My Hands
'Tis Autumn
Where Or When
Who Cares?
With A Song In My Heart
You Go To My Head
And Hundreds More!

The New Real Book - Volume 1 (C, Bb or Eb)

Angel Eyes
Anthropology
Autumn Leaves
Beautiful Love
Bernie's Tune
Blue Bossa
Blue Daniel
But Beautiful
Chain Of Fools
Chelsea Bridge
Compared To What
Darn That Dream
Desafinado
Early Autumn

Eighty One
E.S.P.
Everything Happens To Me
Feel Like Makin' Love
Footprints
Four
Four On Six
Gee Baby Ain't I Good
To You
Gone With The Wind
Here's That Rainy Day
I Love Lucy
I Mean You
I Should Care

I Thought About You
If I Were A Bell
Imagination
The Island
Jersey Bounce
Joshua
Lady Bird
Like Someone In Love
Little Sunflower
Lush Life
Mercy, Mercy, Mercy
The Midnight Sun
Monk's Mood
Moonlight In Vermont

My Shining Hour
Nature Boy
Nefertiti
Nothing Personal
Oleo
Once I Loved
Out Of This World
Pent Up House
Portrait Of Tracy
Put It Where You Want It
Robbin's Nest
Ruby, My Dear
Satin Doll
Search For Peace

Shaker Song
Skylark
A Sleepin' Bee
Solar
Speak No Evil
St. Thomas
Street Life
Tenderly
These Foolish Things
This Masquerade
Three Views Of A Secret
Waltz For Debby
Willow Weep For Me
And Many More!

The New Real Book Play-Along CDs (For Volume 1)

CD #1 - Jazz Classics - Lady Bird, Bouncin' With Bud, Up Jumped Spring, Monk's Mood, Doors, Very Early, Eighty One, Voyage **& More!**
CD #2 - Choice Standards - Beautiful Love, Darn That Dream, Moonlight In Vermont, Trieste, My Shining Hour, I Should Care **& More!**
CD #3 - Pop-Fusion - Morning Dance, Nothing Personal, La Samba, Hideaway, This Masquerade, Three Views Of A Secret, Rio **& More!**
World-Class Rhythm Sections, featuring Mark Levine, Larry Dunlap, Sky Evergreen, Bob Magnusson, Keith Jones, Vince Lateano & Tom Hayashi

The New Real Book - Volume 2 (C, Bb or Eb)

Afro-Centric
After You've Gone
Along Came Betty
Bessie's Blues
Black Coffee
Blues For Alice
Body And Soul
Bolivia
The Boy Next Door
Bye Bye Blackbird
Cherokee
A Child Is Born
Cold Duck Time
Day By Day

Django
Equinox
Exactly Like You
Falling Grace
Five Hundred Miles High
Freedom Jazz Dance
Giant Steps
Harlem Nocturne
Hi-Fly
Honeysuckle Rose
I Hadn't Anyone 'Til You
I'll Be Around
I'll Get By
Ill Wind

I'm Glad There Is You
Impressions
In Your Own Sweet Way
It's The Talk Of The Town
Jordu
Killer Joe
Lullaby Of The Leaves
Manha De Carneval
The Masquerade Is Over
Memories Of You
Moment's Notice
Mood Indigo
My Ship
Naima

Nica's Dream
Once In A While
Perdido
Rosetta
Sea Journey
Senor Blues
September Song
Seven Steps To Heaven
Silver's Serenade
So Many Stars
Some Other Blues
Song For My Father
Sophisticated Lady
Spain

Stablemates
Stardust
Sweet And Lovely
That's All
There Is No Greater Love
'Til There Was You
Time Remembered
Turn Out The Stars
Unforgettable
While We're Young
Whisper Not
Will You Still Be Mine?
You're Everything
And Many More!

The New Real Book - Volume 3 (C, Bb, Eb or Bass clef)

Actual Proof
Ain't That Peculiar
Almost Like Being In Love
Another Star
Autumn Serenade
Bird Of Beauty
Black Nile
Blue Moon
Butterfly
Caravan
Ceora
Close Your Eyes
Creepin'
Day Dream

Dolphin Dance
Don't Be That Way
Don't Blame Me
Emily
Everything I Have Is Yours
For All We Know
Freedomland
The Gentle Rain
Get Ready
A Ghost Of A Chance
Heat Wave
How Sweet It Is
I Fall In Love Too Easily
I Got It Bad

I Hear A Rhapsody
If You Could See Me Now
In A Mellow Tone
In A Sentimental Mood
Inner Urge
Invitation
The Jitterbug Waltz
Just Friends
Just You, Just Me
Knock On Wood
The Lamp Is Low
Laura
Let's Stay Together
Lonely Woman

Maiden Voyage
Moon And Sand
Moonglow
My Girl
On Green Dolphin Street
Over The Rainbow
Prelude To A Kiss
Respect
Ruby
The Second Time Around
Serenata
The Shadow Of Your Smile
So Near, So Far
Solitude

Speak Like A Child
Spring Is Here
Stairway To The Stars
Star Eyes
Stars Fell On Alabama
Stompin' At The Savoy
Sweet Lorraine
Taking A Chance On Love
This Is New
Too High
(Used To Be A) Cha Cha
When Lights Are Low
You Must Believe In Spring
And Many More!

The All Jazz Real Book

Over 540 pages of tunes as recorded by:
Miles, Trane, Bill Evans, Cannonball, Scofield, Brecker, Yellowjackets, Bird, Mulgrew Miller, Kenny Werner, MJQ, McCoy Tyner, Kurt Elling, Brad Mehldau, Don Grolnick, Kenny Garrett, Patitucci, Jerry Bergonzi, Stanley Clarke, Tom Harrell, Herbie Hancock, Horace Silver, Stan Getz, Sonny Rollins, and MORE!

Includes a free CD of many of the melodies
(featuring Bob Sheppard & Friends.). $44 list price.
Available in C, Bb, Eb

The European Real Book

An amazing collection of some of the greatest jazz compositions ever recorded! Available in C, Bb and Eb. $40

- Over 100 of Europe's best jazz writers.
- 100% accurate, composer-approved charts.
- 400 pages of fresh, exciting sounds from virtually every country in Europe.
- Sher Music's superior legibility and signature calligraphy makes reading the music easy.

Listen to FREE MP3 FILES of many of the songs at
www.shermusic.com!

See **www.shermusic.com** for more information, including a complete list of tunes in all our fake books.
To order, call (800) 444-7437 or fax (707) 763-2038

SHER MUSIC JAZZ PUBLICATIONS

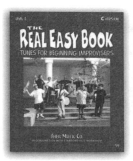

The Real Easy Book Vol. 1
TUNES FOR BEGINNING IMPROVISERS

Published by Sher Music Co. in conjunction with the Stanford Jazz Workshop. $22 list price.

The easiest tunes from Horace Silver, Eddie Harris, Freddie Hubbard, Red Garland, Sonny Rollins, Cedar Walton, Wes Montgomery Cannonball Adderly, etc. Get yourself or your beginning jazz combo sounding good right away with the first fake book ever designed for the beginning improviser. Available in C, Bb, Eb and Bass Clef.

The Real Easy Book Vol. 2
TUNES FOR INTERMEDIATE IMPROVISERS

Published by Sher Music Co. in conjunction with the Stanford Jazz Workshop. Over 240 pages. $29.

The best intermediate-level tunes by: Charlie Parker, John Coltrane, Miles Davis, John Scofield, Sonny Rollins, Horace Silver, Wes Montgomery, Freddie Hubbard, Cal Tjader, Cannonball Adderly, and more! Both volumes feature instructional material tailored for each tune. Perfect for jazz combos! Available in C, Bb, Eb and Bass Clef.

The Real Easy Book Vol. 3
A SHORT HISTORY OF JAZZ

Published by Sher Music Co. in conjunction with the Stanford Jazz Workshop. Over 200 pages. $25.

History text and tunes from all eras and styles of jazz. Perfect for classroom use. Available in C, Bb, Eb and Bass Clef versions.

The Best of Sher Music Co. Real Books
100+ TUNES YOU NEED TO KNOW

A collection of the best-known songs from the world leader in jazz fake books – Sher Music Co.!

Includes songs by: Miles Davis, John Coltrane, Bill Evans, Duke Ellington, Antonio Carlos Jobim, Charlie Parker, John Scofield, Michael Brecker, Weather Report, Horace Silver, Freddie Hubbard, Thelonious Monk, Cannonball Adderley, and many more!

$26. Available in C, Bb, Eb and Bass Clef.

The Serious Jazz Book II
THE HARMONIC APPROACH

By Barry Finnerty, Endorsed by: Joe Lovano, Jamey Aebersold, Hubert Laws, Mark Levine, etc.

- A 200 page, exhaustive study of how to master the harmonic content of songs.
- Contains explanations of every possible type of chord that is used in jazz.
- Clear musical examples to help achieve real harmonic control over melodic improvisation.
- For any instrument. $32. Money back gurantee!

The Serious Jazz Practice Book By Barry Finnerty

A unique and comprehensive plan for mastering the basic building blocks of the jazz language. It takes the most widely-used scales and chords and gives you step-by-step exercises that dissect them into hundreds of cool, useable patterns. Includes CD - $30 list price.

"The book I've been waiting for!" – Randy Brecker.

"The best book of intervallic studies I've ever seen."
– Mark Levine

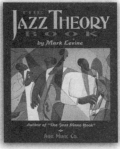

The Jazz Theory Book

By Mark Levine, the most comprehensive Jazz Theory book ever published! $38 list price.

- Over 500 pages of text and over 750 musical examples.
- Written in the language of the working jazz musician, this book is easy to read and user-friendly. At the same time, it is the most comprehensive study of jazz harmony and theory ever published.
- Mark Levine has worked with Bobby Hutcherson, Cal Tjader, Joe Henderson, Woody Shaw, and many other jazz greats.

Jazz Piano Masterclass With Mark Levine
"THE DROP 2 BOOK"

The long-awaited book from the author of "The Jazz Piano Book!" A complete study on how to use "drop 2" chord voicings to create jazz piano magic! 68 pages, plus CD of Mark demonstrating each exercise. $19 list.

"Will make you sound like a real jazz piano player in no time." – Jamey Aebersold

Metaphors For The Musician
By Randy Halberstadt

This practical and enlightening book will help any jazz player or vocalist look at music with "new eyes." Designed for any level of player, on any instrument, "Metaphors For The Musician" provides numerous exercises throughout to help the reader turn these concepts into musical reality.

Guaranteed to help you improve your musicianship. 330 pages – $29 list price. Satisfaction guaranteed!

The Jazz Musicians Guide To Creative Practicing
By David Berkman

Finally a book to help musicians use their practice time wisely! Covers tune analysis, breaking hard tunes into easy components, how to swing better, tricks to playing fast bebop lines, and much more! 150+pages, plus CD. $29 list.

"Fun to read and bursting with things to do and ponder." – Bob Mintzer

The 'Real Easy' Ear Training Book
By Roberta Radley

For all musicians, regardless of instrument or experience, this is the most comprehensive book on "hearing the changes" ever published!

- Covers both beginning and intermediate ear training exercises.
- Music Teachers: You will find this book invaluable in teaching ear training to your students.

Book includes 168 pages of instructional text and musical examples, plus two CDs! $29 list price.

The Jazz Singer's Guidebook By David Berkman
A COURSE IN JAZZ HARMONY AND SCAT SINGING FOR THE SERIOUS JAZZ VOCALIST

A clear, step-by-step approach for serious singers who want to improve their grasp of jazz harmony and gain a deeper understanding of music fundamentals.

This book will change how you hear music and make you a better singer, as well as give you the tools to develop your singing in directions you may not have thought possible.

$26 – includes audio CD demonstrating many exercises.

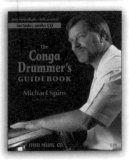